Gallery Books
Editor Peter Fallon

WHAT REMAINS THE SAME

Alvy Carragher

WHAT REMAINS THE SAME

Gallery Books

What Remains the Same
is first published
simultaneously in paperback
and in a clothbound edition
on 18 April 2024.

The Gallery Press
Loughcrew
Oldcastle
County Meath
Ireland

www.gallerypress.com

ISBN 978 1 91133 876 5 *paperback*
     978 1 91133 877 2 *clothbound*

A CIP catalogue record for this book
is available from the British Library.

What Remains the Same receives financial
assistance from the Arts Council.

Contents

for Stephen Murphy,
mo chroí

The hope of accuracy we bring to such tasks is crazy, heartbreaking. And no list could hold what I wanted, for what I wanted was every last thing, every layer of speech and thought, stroke of light on bark or walls, every smell, pothole, pain, crack, delusion, held still and held together — radiant, everlasting.
— Alice Munro, *Lives of Girls and Women*

PART ONE

Split

I dreamt of the girl day after day,
of scrubbing her wounds from my knees,
of walking her to the astounded mouth of the sea,
a ghost in my clenched fist, the river thundering
as she slipped from my body so cleanly.

What more can I tell you?
One of us held on, one of us faltered,
one of us stared at the other treading water.
One of us turned and, turning, found
she could not step away. One of us spoke
and, speaking, found she could not say,
Is this your river flooding my throat?
Is this your thunder cracking my chest?

Background Noise

Maybe I was born for this high room
above the city blinking lullabies of light
but some days when I look at grass
I can't remember the sound of myself.

I've forgotten how to sketch the breeze
and half the things I say are borrowed.
I keep recycling the same old newsfeed
and talking in the presence of my phone.

All day the algorithms mine what's mine,
a future self, pulsing in the background,
but I know the wind wears simple sounds
and I dream the land that broke my fall.

Forgive Me

It's easy to think I'm healing
the days are so quiet,
but I keep coming down
with the same thoughts.

All day I'm trying to let go
of the country in my chest
but it takes such a time
to get close to anything.

I wake from long corridors;
fading violets bruise my legs
from walking into walls,
bumping into furniture.

It's hard to grasp a room
when each holds the shadow
of an old home, another country.

Whenever I open my head
the past has shifted;
impossible to shrink,
it grows inside me,
and I try to forgive
what it says.

And now this feverish
calling up of alphabet,
I fix myself to the page,
finding only the same questions.

What kind of archaeology is this?
Back among the artefacts
the past stamps its foot
like a small child.

Origin Story

It begins with you, the name given later,
syllables swimming in the dark of mother.
Do your cells remember floating ahead,
how you forgot a coat here, a friend there?
It's remarkable what fades, what remains,
scents like lavender rubbed into wrists,
fear rubbed deep into temples. Begin there,
with fear, a thing you take in both hands
and give freely, just like the ones before.
Long ago a horrible thing happened. Begin
with your grandmother's pain, pass on
all that scares you — walking off the edge,
meeting strangers, inhabiting the word *no*.
Begin with your father looking at you
as if he expects to feel more, your mother
bent over the cot, checking your pulse,
worrying up and down the stairs with milk.
It's as if she's given birth to a little judge
and now she must tend to her. Begin with facts,
if you can find any. Do not trust the photographs;
let time work strange rhythms around you;
muddle past jobs, cities, schools. Memories
move through you, fish-like, glinting
and disappearing. Begin with the years
spent surviving in your head, how you left
through the opening in a prayer, back when
they ran through you like source code.
Begin with how you hurt the ones you love.
It stings. Begin elsewhere. Begin with rain,
with the earth holding you. Here is a field.
Let this be your beginning, your whole heart

      witnessing.

Field Notes

I go to the honeysuckle, pink flowers trapped
in our mouths as Granny answers the door;
a phone rings endlessly in the hall. In the big field
dandelions sour our fingers. We snip nettles
to make the soup from *Peadar Pluaise*. Leaves float
in hot water, wilted outlines of their former selves.
Uncle John drinks the lot, says we're great chefs.
We worry it will rash his stomach, and hide.

Our pale faces age like squat primroses
looking for light; a willow tree curtains the earth
where I love to read. We traipse through fields;
wild strawberries and blackberries grow with no help
from anyone; deer tracks lead downstream to a sea
of bluebells and we rest in a glen where druids
used to sing; oaks filter the world to a mossy glow
as we squish sloes on warm necks and squeal.

We race, crawl under hawthorn into our field;
blue-headed thistles cling to our jumpers.
We peel back green buds of sleeping poppies,
search for ink caps among daisies and dew, unearth
dark-tasting mushrooms; they stain stew purple.
We bake tarts with apples from trees that tap the roof;
we stand on cold bathroom tiles where Mammy makes
crab apple jelly by straining gloop through old tights
in the bathtub. A plastic bucket traps golden liquid
which sets in clear jars. On toast it tastes luminous.

The Famine House

Walk out across the fields,
no simple paths, no gates left open;

        wear a good coat, something *insistent,*
        there's nothing but hard rain out here.

Haul yourself over fences, thickets,
stand against the pummel and tug;

        listen for water, follow streams,
        keep an eye out for remnants, stone.

When you come to the rubble
trace the outline of a house, a hearth;

        look closer —
        a woman bends to tend the pot.

In it the last of her garden takes shape,
filling her one room with herbs and sky.

        She's collecting herself for a journey,
        barefoot across the land; she's leaving

the only home she's ever known,
the smell of soft peat on her hands.

Wildflowers

My mother sends me to pick wildflowers at night
for the centre of our table, my sisters in their beds cry out
as I slip into the dark, the morning dithering before me.
I ignore the flowers, fix my eyes on a remote spot,
move towards it. *Let me be invisible, let me walk under*
the last bit of moon, don't let the sun put her eyes
on my swollen face, don't let anyone see how much it hurts
to leave, just give me an hour to collect myself.

I measure the fields behind me
until I'm far enough away to curl up in a ditch,
to rest, to eat the bread from my pockets —
the last time I will taste this flavour. Bread is different
everywhere else; even if it's not I will imagine it is,
forever wanting this loaf that tastes of the field beyond
our house where I stopped to look back at our cottage,
a dark blot in the night. If I had seen my brother
at the window, my sisters at the door, I'd have dropped
to the ground, pulled up the wildflowers with my teeth
and crawled back to them, said I was sleepwalking.

I dream as I go, milky white thoughts slipping in and out,
lines and lines of poetry and old songs that meander off
into nothing, boreens back to the dead — my grandfather
shrunk and dignified, how my mother buckled,
her legs slipping out from under her, until she was down
on her knees, sorrier than I had ever seen her.
I was too young to understand, ran outside to tell the others
as if it were any other piece of news, their wide eyes
orbiting me as mysterious as his lifeless body,
how I thought about my mother ending up in that bed,
how I too would lie down in it eventually.

The first lines came after that. I used them to hook
my mother out of sadness, wrote words for my father too

but they didn't crack the hardest part of his skull.
I gave up, left them with him, with her. Sometimes
you've to give up and take the last artery out of childhood
with its brambles and wildflowers, the spot where I flew
over the handlebars, so that when I walk past
that hiccup in the road I see the doctor's hands,
how she said it was nothing, though there was blood.

Most journeys have companions.
Mine are these, and the memory of rain pounding
the roof of the attic, a prayer I refuse to say
though I used to believe it. When I lived through
my near death it was there, pacing up and down
my mind, urging me to hang on, take a step further,
past churches and schools, all the legends
that stoop over my life, history hounding my heels.

Every few towns I've to stop and ask for help.
At first it is impossible. I am shy, taught not to ask
for anything, but soon I forget. Shoulders back, I open
my mouth and speak. I press my feet into every line
of a restless map, grow older in cities that hold my hand
loosely. My home wavers behind me, its grey sky
indifferent to where I go next. My feet slap the concrete
of new continents, fluorescent lighting, logos loom
on every surface, addicts collapse and their wails,
raw, ready to take the one road home —

the bramble, the scabbed knee. Mud swallows
my footsteps, rain buries my markings,
headaches cloud round me. I'm back at the stove,
back in the garden, back reading my brother to sleep.
How can I escape? Their names are faint.
Sometimes I fall asleep, whispering to them,
know they're whispering back, each in their own way.

Our blood reaches through invisible lines —
like roads, like boreens, like poems tugging us down
into ourselves, trembling. Is there a way
to lay this down, to stand in the field beyond our house,
to face the wildflowers, my mother on her knees?

PART TWO

What Remains the Same

It doesn't matter which version you've heard,
whether they become swans or squat pigeons.

> Flip a coin. Let's say six or seven brothers,
> give them any old feathers, eyes that glint.

Count the years since their mother passed,
place each name on their sister's feverish lips.

> Details are immaterial, ornaments hung
> on the narrow branch of story. Let them fall.

What remains is a sister, alone,
trying to break her brothers' curse,

> stitching garments from thick nettles
> that break and blister her skin.

She must swallow pain, remain silent.
This is the shape of her life.

> What love, what duty compels her?
> If we forget for a moment the brothers,

if we look at her red eyes, her set mouth,
if we take her ruined hands in ours,

> if we press an ear to her silence,
> can we forgive ourselves this story?

Mallacht

My grandmother told a story
about a man who put a curse on our family.
I imagine a silver beard with puckered skin,
stepping out of the forest, laying his curse
at my grandmother's feet, *a son haunted by water.*
Nobody ever said what my father had done
to deserve it. All my life water followed us.
In a country of rain my father believed
his own damnation. Every burst pipe and wet day
came back to a stranger laying his words
at my grandmother's feet, how she chose
to pick them up, pass them on, give them power.

Reduction

I keep writing my mother into kitchens
as if I cannot imagine her another way —
cake cooling on counter, knife on table,
the disturbance of us in the background.
A life in dollhouse proportions —
a stove, a child, four walls pressing in on her,
never the sharp turn of her head,
never her dark and restless silences.
Maybe this is how I want her preserved,
bending over ovens, crooning to the radio,
a careful sketch contained by the page.
How can I write the word mother
and not reduce her to the idea of one?
Like berries cooked down to a sweet jam
after all their wild and irresistible living.

Creatures

My mother never asked for
  puppies, kittens, child after child;
    all our helpless heads turned towards her.

Season after season she tends to us,
  slams down food, loses control,
    returns to us full of apology.

Something in the air is splintered.
  We fix our hungry love upon the pets;
    safer, wet eyes, soft paws,
      what can they do but look at you?

We copy what we've learnt;
  they flinch before we strike them;
    we return to them, begging forgiveness,

whole litters bagged and drowned,
  dirty work, buried in the field.
    She refuses to show us the graves

but saves one from every litter,
  gives it to us, framing it as a test
    to determine our capacity for caring.

My kitten leaves me,
  nothing for him in the dark shed,
    padfoot, grief warden, hungry orphan,

I try to lure him home, desperate.
  Maybe no part of me will ever mother.
    How can I, when he once pressed his nose
      to my fingertip in complete surrender?

Aimsir

Ours was a house where we lived like weathervanes,
knew to position our bodies in line with the wind,
could read the mood of a room by the angle of a frying pan,
like sundials measuring light by the shadows we threw.

We hid ourselves in cupboards, trees, the eaves of attics,
backs pressed against walls, moving watchfully
through the days, instincts finely tuned to the way
air moved through our parents. It was a lesson in dignity,
how it is straight-backed and miserable, how it rarely
means survival, how one day you must abandon it.

Like the day a storm broke in my mother and I felt
all the rage in her coming for me. She wanted to hit me
for what I had done. I flung myself on the floor
before she could lash out, knowing it would stop her anger
thickening. My sisters gathered, outlines in the doorway,
performing their outrage, locked in the pantomime.
I whimpered at my mother's feet, but it was not
my mother before me, only a young girl trembling.

For years the poem ended there, a polished half-truth,
an erasure. It was easier to assign pain to the perpetual
passages of girlhood, but I've carried it much further,
shrinking my mother, myself. I'll say this about what's
missing: it was the year she finally left my father,
hoping I wouldn't leave her. I was seventeen, the eldest
daughter on the doorstep of departure, almost a woman,
a body curled around my mother's swinging foot.

When Nobody Was Watching

We were violent sisters
who grabbed each other by the hair
and swung with all our strength.
No strangers to kicking heads or stomachs,
fists pummelling. Experts at pinching,
twisting. We wielded elbows, knees,
sometimes a skipping rope, a stick.
We fought, we fled.

I'm not sure what other sisters teach each other.
I've learnt to forgive what she's forgiven —
how I rose in deepest hurt to lunge for her ankle,
force her back down to the dirt.

Songbird

My father was a hum
at the other end of his workshop,
keeping time with the radios,
one in each corner, battered and dusty,
antennae made sturdy with tape.

My sister hit all the wrong notes,
left them writhing on the kitchen floor.
My father picked them up, opening
his mouth to let loose a songbird. It burst
from his chest, taking flight among teenagers
and tea towels, potatoes boiling on the hob;
even the dog sat mesmerized as it soared.

Until my father snatched it from the air,
cramming it into his mouth, swallowing
it whole. At night I heard it again, moving
through the walls. I wanted to ask why he kept it
from us but I said nothing and, each day,
the songbird hummed madly behind his teeth.

Merrow

Some days my mother was so weak
I wanted to leave her. Imagined walking out
the door, across the fields, as far as I could get.

I started running just to be alone in the world,
away from our house with its twisted spine
and the dog with his hurt eyes.

I ran the brutal miles, up the Silvermines,
through farmers' fields, the grass and mud.
Built to move across the earth, I was a land animal.

My mother was not. Rooms were a shape she struggled
to fill, required a rigidness that did not come naturally.
She was part water, part fish. Seaweed parted for her.

Jellyfish made way. She swaggered through water,
cut strokes sharp and clean. In the shallows
I was embarrassed by my weak limbs, rarely brave
enough to lift my feet clean off the land.

My mother was suddenly weightless.
Nothing mattered, only the breath, the rhythm,
her tiny trapped head in the vastness.

The Dreamhouse

When I went to my mother for help
she said there was a way to hold on,
no matter what he said or did.

You go inside, she said, deep down
to the dreamhouse. Focus on something small,
a fingernail, a scar, a freckle. Let it blur
until the front door begins to materialize,
a brass knob, a knocker, a letterbox.
Wait for it to feel solid. Then enter.

You had to go layer by intricate layer,
every inch mattered, details were important,
the exact colour of a teapot, the curtains.
You had to build each room as if it were real,
as if you could press your hands to the windows.

I focused on the crease between his eyes.
He stormed and I footstepped closer.
He raged and I slipped through the door.
He could not see where I had gone,
only that I was no longer with him.

When I was in that house
with its thick carpets and sunshine walls —
my mother, my sisters, my brother, all safe —
once I was there I'd run through the rooms
to make sure he wasn't hiding anywhere.

Responsibility

I used to think it was one of us
who caused my mother all that grief,
tearing ourselves from her body,
leaving her weak.

But that's too obvious,
the kind of thing we speak about.
I decided on my father,
only to realize they had found each other
already in pain, and there's a difference
between deepening and creating.

Hers is an ancient hurt returning
from the corridors of childhood
where her mother slept in the front room
to protect her children from the outside.

My mother slept at the back of the house,
up creaking flights of stairs, country dark,
the moon too thin to make a difference.
Nobody would have heard if she tried to call out
but she would not have tried.

Not my mother.

She grew silent, shown to huddle
beneath coarse blankets, given prayers.

How many Hail Marys floated up in the dark?

The whole house deaf
to what it was that went on
in the rooms of its daughters.

One Way of Looking At It

There's nothing unusual about my mother's story,
even that she turned to her children with it.
Nobody else cared to listen so the child in her
cried out to the children she raised. *I'm hurt too.*

How is it that one person's pain can pass
from body to body? Like the birthday party game
where a parcel moves through the circle, music plays,
some children linger, hoping the music stops,

so they can unwrap a layer, find what's hidden.
When the parcel came my way I jerked my hands,
joking, flinging it at the next person, causing laughter.
I could not bear to hold one more burning secret.

Responsibility 2

I knew a man
they put a war inside;
it wasn't there when he was born,
no matter what they say.

I heard they gave it to him
before first words.
He called it internal bruising.

Once his spine was soft
as anybody else's,
then day turned dark
and his years were bare roads.

Nobody cooed or rocked
the pram, he told me this —
how later all he could remember
is a feeling so heavy it was empty.
He never saw beyond it.

He was little.
You have to understand how small.
That was back when we,
I mean *we*, beat him
for his own good. A lesson.
He was blue and cold as tender meat.

I'm telling you he grew up hard.
He had a mind like a clenched fist —
it held on to anything that hurt.

I'm saying he survived
with a laugh that cut the air
from under anyone who touched him.

I knew a man, and then another.
Scar after scar.

I saw women try to hold him,
I saw black liquid drink him up.
I saw children try to raise him —
faces like echoes, they sat at his feet.

I knew a man *we* put a war inside;
it wasn't there when he was born,
no matter what we say.

Quarry

In a house built from desire a young girl gives;
nothing is easy when even the walls hunger.

On days it's too much she climbs the quarry,
dangles her body over the edge, faces sheer rock,

bone-scraping scree. Her hands grip the land's
sharp tongue as she chews the names of her saints.

She lets eternity pass. Below the hunt plays out,
horns sound and her name is the heart of the blast.

Her thoughts acquire a new taste,
blown open by the wind, scattered, wild,

her eyes cloud with one recurring image,
scurrying dogs, a fox so slight it's barely there.

Nobody Speaks Her Language Outside Dreams

Nobody speaks her language outside dreams.
All they ever say is speak up, speak up.
She's surprised they cannot hear her thoughts
stride across the classroom and go aching out the window
to sing among birds, fizz between telephone wires.

In photographs she is expressionless, except her eyes
which do not see beyond the shutter closing
its dark mouth around her pale and serious face.

Something is wrong with her; of that much they're sure.
What kind of girl cannot answer her own mother?

In the mornings her mouth is dry,
the room stiff; she plants her feet, willing roots
to sprout from her sole, tunnel down through knots
of wood, deep into dirt and worms.

The great spirit of her body is full of cloud and mulch,
it speaks the language of sun-soaked cat, of petal wilt,
of grass seed sifted between fingers.

Her body is a cover, her mind a choir,
she doesn't need to close her eyes
to see what gathers behind lids.

When light slants through windows she wonders why
the others do not turn their heads to look at dust motes;
she thinks her grandfather must live among those specks.

At night she's rarely scared. The room's pitch black
but her body knows tricks. One by one
she pulls white rabbits from her long dark hair
and sets them free, these glowing creatures circle her bed
performing leap after phenomenal leap.

Bedtime Stories

Sometimes they drank wine and loved us
until the kitchen felt swollen and bloated,
stories pouring from stemmed glasses,
mouths black holes as they shaped myths,
gave us roles, delighting in their creations.

It happened by the fireplace on bath night,
three heads of long hair combed out to dry,
our backs to the flickering light. We began
unravelling. O Story, she came for us,
and we took up the mantle, one by one.

I would sit there still. Nightdress tugged
down over knees, chin resting, eyes fixed
on these morphing figures. My whole body
thirsty for more, how untouchable we were
when they drank the dark, shining liquid.

PART THREE

Stampede

I've never heard the story
where three motionless sisters
stand at the boundary
between this world and the next
but they are there anyway
waiting for bullocks to charge.

Through a gap in the hedge
they see blunt heads heaving
towards their slight bodies.
They form a determined line.

Maybe you've stood like that,
waiting for thundering muscle
to do what it will
to the gentle organ of your life.

Is there a song for these sisters
who came for this stampede
of hooves and hot breath,
the sky a mess above them.

A stranger might wonder
if they're trying to get themselves killed,
but a stranger cannot hear
what they're asking.

Can brute animals hold themselves back?
If we die will they be sorry?
Are clouds thumbprints of the gods?
Will birds sing over our bodies?

I've never heard the story
where these sisters take flight,
gone in one sudden movement

as if tied by a single thought,
disappearing over brambles into sky.

Is there a song for these sisters
who know when to stand their ground
and when to give it up?

If you listen
all you'll hear is laughter;
maybe you've laughed like that,
letting joy do what it will
to heal the ruptured earth.

In Other Words

The car was a frosted red ornament.
Mother rose early to start the engine,
boil kettles, pour warm water on the windows;

ice cracked, and the car burst into hum.
In the back seat I fogged the glass,
refusing to look at my sisters waving me off.

Alone at the school gates I pulled up my socks,
smoothed the pleats on my stiff, grey pinafore,
hurried by the wall where big boys loomed.

Nobody told me what I was doing there
or how long I'd have to stay. Nothing made sense:
who to be without my sisters, the alphabet.

I couldn't say L without M-N-O-P or understand
how separate things might sometimes form a whole,
that letters lived both inside and outside words.

Nobody told me there were two languages,
or they did, and I didn't know what language meant.
Suddenly there were two words for everything —

window and *fuinneog*, door and *doras*, Alvy and *Ailbhe*.
All winter the first name shook me from sleep
and, in the car, I slipped the new name over my head.

The Newcomers

Sometimes the cows
graze behind our school,

the black and white
splotchwork of their bodies,

fresh against the patchwork
of fields and sheds.

We gather
under the high wall

until a great head leans over,
big velvety pools.

We stand before her
as others have stood.

Down through the centuries
one stranger faces another

across a divide, time distils.
The imperceptible passes

as one hand reaches
to touch the other,

as warm breath
blesses that hand.

Among Treetops

Our apple trees touch at the top
as if having grown up separately
they decided to turn to each other
before it was too late.

I climb to where they meet,
light enough to inch along
their thinnest branches,
not for the apples, but the thrill
of stepping from one tree to another,
testing the strength with my foot,
balancing, aeroplane arms steady
in the land of wind and branches.

Coming down to earth scares me.
I call my mother, she climbs halfway,
Why go up there if you're so afraid?
Though she knows. Which of us doesn't?
You never lose the taste for sky walking.

Let me show you. Close your eyes.
It is late Autumn; most leaves have fallen.
Climb with me, up, up out of the earth;
feel how cold it is here; touch a wet leaf
to your cheek. The sky is only inches away.

Sunday Prayers

And if I speak of waiting
then I'm speaking of the church in Gortanumera
with its sermons and communions and stained glass,
how the minutes stood still each Sunday
as I endured the ritual although, I imagine,
the church is abandoned now and full of empty pews.

And if I speak of empty
then I'm speaking of prayers about fathers
and forgiveness, despite Mary being the backbone
of the rosary, the one relatable character
in the Stations of the Cross. She stood before me
in stone, on the left side of the church,
where only the women and children could sit.

And if I speak of that side of the church
then I'm speaking of our hearts, slightly left of centre,
tilting our bodies back towards our mothers.

And if I speak of mothers
then I'm speaking of mine and the silence she taught me.
Perhaps it's a trick handed down to all daughters —
how to keep words firmly under our tongues
until they've grown long and sickening roots.

And if I speak of tongues
then I'm speaking mostly of my own,
counting the backs of my teeth
as the priest went on and on,
his sermon lasting until he landed
on the words he felt needed to be said.

And if I speak of words
then I'm speaking of searching
for a place to rest my head

where the truth will come in streams of light
tinted red and purple and blue by stained glass,
just about vivid enough to touch.

The Summer Our Bodies Began to Speak

for Casey Armstrong

It was the hour of long limbs,
of growing in and out of shoes,
of sun-streaked hair, of first kiss,
of listing the boys we would
and most certainly wouldn't.
It was the hour of sent to play,
of long days and endless fields,
of chaining daisies, limp bracelets.
It was the hour of inventing ways
to avoid becoming our mothers,
of reporting back, bloated with newness,
after games of kiss chase or truth and dare,
one tongue pushing against another.
How we squirmed at the prickle
of our desires, and blamed
the boys who pinned us down.
We let them, and they let us
let them, all of us wanting to belong.
When we got tired of all this
it was the hour of comparison,
of filling taut bellies with air,
of making round moons of ourselves,
T-shirts pulled up to our chests.
We catalogued our parts, lining up,
labelling fattest, thinnest, tallest.
We could describe it all, blondest hair,
straightest teeth, thickest eyebrows.
Our palms were next, scrutinized,
so we might know how many children,
who would die young, who would suffer.
We were sure we wanted answers.

Elvis and the River Goddess

We lived along the River Shannon —
the bed of a drowned goddess,
her power dissolving, seeping into water,
her voice a blur of current and weather.

We lay on her banks, freckling,
school shirts loose and billowing,
dipping our toes in her shallows,
feet searching out smooth stones,
hungry for her impenetrable strength,
though we knew of her moods.

Back when they were a thing
Leah had pink lipgloss
that made her lips bigger,
the sting of the swell.
We took turns smearing it on,
deciding who had the best lips
as Elvis smoked cigarettes in silence.

He was one of us for years,
then on the outskirts —
when it's over it's over —
his face in our cloud, dissolving.

Our nettle mouths
forming black holes
the night he threw himself
into her darkest current,
only to be pulled out shivering,
as all around water surged
toward our wide-open mouths.

The Unanswered Question

A lighter up each sleeve, she fell in love
most weeks, snuck out to smoke with anyone
who stood still long enough. A frequenter
of petrol stations, her twang never caught
a lilt but hung like an exclamation mark,
strutting through tables, taboos. Laughing,
as I slid in and out of uniform and hid
the straps of tatty bras. Some days she couldn't
hold a smile, fled classrooms wordlessly,
teachers shrugged or shook their heads
as I raced after her. Nights, she called about
homework, serious, wanting answers.
Weekends, she'd insist on staying over
to flick through drawers, root out anything
half-hidden. Nothing made her flinch.

Later she spoke in her old voice of new things —
men, many cruelties. She'd call out of the blue,
wanting answers: if she should leave, if I forgave
my mother for staying. Inevitably she'd describe
the one moment, the constant reel —
standing on the stairs, worried about exams,
her parents arguing above her, the usual violence,
nothing that made her look up, what she wouldn't give
to see it clearly, if her father pushed or her mother fell,
too late when her mother hurtled towards her,
there was no time to catch the falling body.
And so she'd ask if I'd read some theory yet
to explain why she stood there, frozen.

A Stranger in the Air

I left at nineteen — goodbye country —
empty shirts on the clothesline waving,
crumpled arms caught in the wind,
the green of my heart blurring to grey;
there was nothing beyond me but sky,
a great blue intention I flew through
to the land of blockbuster films,
an accent I'd mimicked in the garden.
The first time I crossed the Atlantic
my geography was crooked, Louisiana
just a shape on the map, a kind of shoe,
I winged toward, a bruised suitcase
full of everything I'd ever known.

The woman beside me on the plane
was a proud Texan, a homebird returning.
She had twin girls, about fourteen, sleeping
in the other aisle, an arm's length away,
slumped together, matching pink pillows,
a pair of earbuds split between them;
they slept in the arms of the same song.

The woman's twang was a lullaby.
She wanted to know about my mother
and kept one eye always on her daughters,
a Mary Poppins purse open on her lap,
the gold clasp undone; she never rooted,
items seemed to float into her hands, gum,
wipes, all packed in neat compartments,
conjured at the slightest stir, the gentlest whim.
She had questions that she didn't ask.
They trundled by like the food trolley,
bumping against our aisle, never stopping.
Just as well, what answers could I give?

For the last leg we flew in silence.
When I dozed she slipped a pillow
under my head, the lightest touch.
I woke to find it there. We'd landed,
no longer suspended above the earth.
She hurried her girls, checking bags, seats.
I returned the pillow and thanked her.
She said it was nothing, one day someone
would do the same for her daughters.
She left, steering them onwards,
bartering with the universe, with God,
or whatever faith we give such prayers.

Bookmarks

I leave dog-ears, others leave receipts,
sweet wrappers, tickets elsewhere
and, once, a note typed on an index card
deep in a book called *Heart Songs*,
a selection of young girls' diaries,
a yellowing paperback buried in a pile.
The cover from a steel engraving
shows two girls strewn on the grass,
the dreamy half-gaze, picking out notes
on a violin, a mandolin. Such music.

The note leans between diaries,
printed in the clean script of a typewriter,
adjustments made by overlapping letters,
and a patch or two of corrective fluid.
I don't scratch to see what's underneath,
preferring to preserve these male sentences,
quite unlike those of the girls it rests between —
their thoughts overflow, his script so thin,
as if he starts with the end in mind,
as if writing too much might erase it.

He says, *Susan, as the evening wore on,*
I found that I loved you all the more.
I trace street names on a map
as he walks through a long evening.
It's the first firm flush of spring.
He is humbled not by any leaf or bud
but this new love accumulating.
He thrums along stretches of pavement,
carrying Susan with him, not seeing the sky
purple and pink, not seeing light dim,
because for this man on this walk
the light is no longer interesting.

There is a woman caught in his throat
and he's writing, and rewriting her,
so that when he bends his head to type,
he gives her his heart song, so simple
and practical. She presses it between pages,
holding their place in the borrowed world
where it remains dog-eared, timeless, rustling.

Socrates Likes to Talk Philosophy at the Taverna

It must be the burden of his name, all this talk
of philosophy, which seems to be just talk. He's full
of chat, never short of a story, maybe even lonely.
He reminds me of old men sipping pints on worn out
stools, though he drinks ouzo, and this is his taverna.
Light pours in, illuminating checked tablecloths
and wooden floors, window sills painted blue
to match the sea, shells dangle from threads —
he collects them when he hunts, harpooning tuna,
then drifting in search of the sea's pink trinkets.
All day I work the nearby bar, wipe counters, pour
cold coffees and rub mint to make mojitos bloom.

He brings me things. Once it's a dessert called sweet.
I say it's grainy like caviar. Afterwards he calls it sweet caviar.
He holds out fresh salt in his palm, picked from the rocks
that morning, limpets still breathing in their shells.
Each gift comes with a Greek word. I take these parcels
of language, eat my fill. He brings wild capers, arms raw
with scratches. He followed goats across the mountain
to find them. He will use the leaves for salad, pickle
the stalks, use each part of the plant, not just the caper.
He fills silence and I soak in his sentences.

Slowly he is building a house in the mountains.
His mother says to really live you must have
your own home and a wife. He looks out to sea
as she says this. What is it he sees out there?
Maybe America. Most days he mentions it,
how he saved fifty thousand dollars because he never
went to the movies and didn't know how to spend it.
He remembers an Irish woman in Brooklyn,
how he stood in the streetlight and threw pebbles
at her window (as if in one of those movies

he never went to see). She sat inside, terrified.
I imagine him young and burning in a land of concrete.

One night he picks up my drunk housemate at the bar,
takes her down a red dirt road to his half-built home.
She escapes his kiss, refuses to give him what he wants.
Eventually he drives her home. I sit on the floor and listen
to her story. It's impossible to connect my old romantic
to this truth. Everything feels tired and dirty. I eat
in the taverna when he's not there, stare at the green knot
of capers in the bowl, then out at the sea.

Aftermath

The places you're sent look so ordinary —
an office, a chair, a waiting room. Mute interiors.
In therapy press white tissues to your dry eyes
as she lists the ways the system can destroy you.

She says you seem in control, maybe she expects
hair falling out in clumps, clothes unkempt.
It is not enough to sit here with your made-up face,
hands folded in your lap as if this is an interview.

Speaking, you reduce him to a violent word,
in erasing him, you erase parts of yourself.
Wasn't there an hour when you found him
beautiful? Didn't you shave wanting him?

What about the days after? You laugh and eat,
never miss a single day of work or college.
Nobody prepares you for your own strength;
it sits on your shoulders, muttering accusations.

When you tell the story everything happens to you;
it only confuses people if you say anything else.
But you repeat it too many times; the past disappears.
You've become the story. Sleeping, it circles you,

the words won't leave your head, they take root
in your skull, you must live with their terrible flowers.
All you really remember, besides his startling teeth,
is that you wanted to hurt him. That much was mutual.

Ruptures

You're basking outside in the sunshine —
a cup of tea, books, and a tatty pillow.
It's nice to see some things stay the same
though you wear your hair differently now
and your freckles are more apparent.

A tub of peanut butter sits absently to one side.
Last year I watched you eat it from a spoon
on a video chat and was reminded of us
sneaking peanut butter from the kitchen
and spooning it straight from the jar.

When you were born I remember the thrill
of skidding down hospital halls, pushing
through big double doors to get to you.
We threw ourselves across our mother's stomach,
rupturing something. She stayed calm and pale
as she let us cradle you, taught us how to be gentle.

Sister, I slip your name into conversations
though I have not told you anything in so long,
you, who once knew everything.
There seems to be no way for us to speak
without all the old hurt showing up,
making us both sound backward and ugly.

I cannot tell you what it means to be gentle.
Back then it was easy. *Keep still, support the head.*
There's just so much more to it now.

Testimony

My story became a footnote on a wet day,
a character reference for the man who hurt me.
They needed a line of neat and tidy facts
and I was a woman folding and unfolding.

I only half understand this part,
but I'll tell you anyway.
My soul was barely touching my body.

A word like soul doesn't belong
in the courtroom. It disturbs the clear air,
sounds drunk and disorderly. But it matters.

It had me by the fingertips.
That fragile thing had not abandoned
my body completely. Not this time.

I sat in the confession box.
There is a proper name for it,
I know. What I'm saying is:
that it felt as if I had to give everything,
that I would need to be forgiven.

My memory was a dark bleat.
I raised my hand over the bible,
swore to tell the truth,
the whole truth, and nothing but it.

The joke was absolute.

What did I remember about being seven?
I was younger than that
when I gave up on God, whole truths.

Bearing the Gifts

Do you remember when your mother died?
We had no gifts for the altar, no symbols of hers;
it was too far to drive back, stranded as we were,
in a town halfway between her first and last lives.

We swept through the rented house, borrowing objects,
pillaging rosary beads, a wooden rocking horse,
a framed picture of the sea. You blessed each one
with sudden meanings, conjured ceremonial words.

Who amongst us would not bow their head and listen,
as each found object was placed at the altar, reverently?
You spoke as if she were sitting there, front and centre,
her face announcing some harsh and final verdict.

Mourning Song

When days buckle and strain
I remember your bowed head
against a bald and brainless sky.
I've forgotten your face.

What's between us speaks
only in dreams. I see a blackbird,
your sudden death. Morning
shakes me by the shoulders.

Your grief hurls itself
at daughter after daughter.
Who falters? Who stares back
as stubborn as oak?

A clot of clamped-down
thoughts, a dark blot rising.
But he's your father. A catch-all
phrase. A forgive-me-what.

Nothing happened
if nothing got written down.
I worry that, without testimony,
your daughters dissolve.

I'm not built to carry your grief.
You hurt one way, I hurt the other.
You're a splinter, I'm an absence.
I stay on my side of the ocean.

There's a hymn you sang once
about a good daughter.
When I can't sleep
she asks why I betray her.

What kind of daughter cannot daughter,
and what is daughtering?
What kind of father cannot father,
and what is fathering?

This much I know — when you die
I will not bury you.
Father, I'll patch my thoughts.
I'll whistle for the blackbird.

Mother Speaks Across Oceans

It's the deep sigh of midwinter
when she calls to say her mother is dead.
We're in familiar waters. The intimacy
of her voice after so long. Ocean in my ear.
I ask if they made peace. A pause.
Before the end her mother apologized
for not seeing. It has to be enough.
She's just glad that place isn't a place
anymore. I guess she means girlhood.
My mind moves through cold corridors
to a child's bed. Ocean in my throat.
She describes the final hours —
how she refused sleep, somehow knowing
this was her mother's last hour.
She was the only one to witness
her mother fixate on the light.
I don't believe a word of it. Her stamp
is all over the details. It's like a storybook —
colourful, triumphant. A cartoon death,
a ghost in the wrong shoes, singing off-key.
Ocean in my chest. She's relieved it's over.
I say I don't think grief works that way;
there's nothing dismissible in its hollow vowels,
slumped shoulders. The line is silent.
Ocean in my hands. Her voice, again,
an anecdote. It's as if she didn't hear me.
This happened once before and long ago.
I gave up speaking. I let her words enter.
It didn't matter what I said. She spoke
over me. Her voice rising like the tide.

PART FOUR

Library

Sometimes I wonder why she brought us there
so religiously. She was young and thwarted
but she knew to do that much, to show us books
full of lives other than the one we were living.
Maybe all some people can give you is a way out.
Maybe forgiveness is understanding that's enough.

Look, I read for thirty years and ended up here.
A life built from books. I've turned myself
inside out and nobody died or pricked a finger.
Imagine this, I was once so scared I wouldn't speak;
there was a wall between what I felt and others heard.
I couldn't translate until I pressed pen to paper.

Here was my mother tongue. I put down my life
and walked through the covers to another.

The First Poem

It wasn't written
in ancient calligraphy
or etched on tall stones.

It wasn't spoken
in hushed tones
underneath the stars;
there was no bonfire
leaping in the dark.

All we can ever know
is that we missed it,
busy feeding ourselves
and building things
while it was happening
at the mouth of a river.

The clouds showed up,
the grass nodded its head,
the wind said a few words
as the poem passed through.

It was only later
when we came to the water
and stood in the shallows
that we felt its absence.

We did what we always do
and got down on our knees
to try to capture it

but the first poem
was deep in the ocean
and clear light ran
through our fingers.

The Calligrapher's Instructions

When the sky turns murky and deep
break open the ink,

let sentences lead you
out of the fog and fury of the day;

knit words darkly across the page,
each letter matters,

determined downward strokes,
upward feathery ticks;

angle your body to fit
the hunched shoulders of our alphabet.

If your hand cramps
loosen your grip,

waggle your fingers,
make spiders in the air;

should someone interrupt
give yourself back to the page;

under a narrowing sky
lift your pen against silence.

Mornings

The dishwasher sings its ordinary hymn,
here in the utterly changeable act of living.
Each breath keeps one singular soul alive,
and we are instruments needling the dark.

Here in the utterly changeable act of living,
amid the great arrangements of the world,
we are instruments needing the dark,
stitching the facts of our suffering closer.

Amid the great arrangements of the world
we try to thread these tapestries of light,
stitching the facts of our suffering closer.
What is happening outside our windows?

We try to thread these tapestries of flight.
It begins to look patterned, but that's not so.
What's happening outside our windows?
The news comes in bullets. Cities stripped.

It begins to look patterned, but that's not so.
Mornings, children bruise and break.
The news comes in bullets. Cities stripped.
We've lost count of the missing bodies.

Mourning children, bruised, broken.
Will the earth keen? Will the moon rise?
We've lost count of the missing bodies,
trains whistle souls across tired borders.

Will the earth keen? Will the moon rise,
shimmering over many rubbled towns,
as trains whistle souls across tired borders.
Our oldest pains. Our ancient sorrows.

Shivering over many rubbled towns,
we are instruments kneeling in the dark.
Our oldest pains. Our ancient sorrows.
Here. An utterly changeable act. Living.

One Day We Will All Be Ancients

Our gut rot and bad backs forgotten,
our dust scattered, our feuds buried in the orchard
beneath Arja's woolly socks and the earth's final
bottle of 7UP, both refusing to decompose.

Our poorest decisions won't be
so much as a note in the margins,
our laughter an mp3 that crackles
and rasps from ageing speakers.

Not a single memory will remain
of the extra slices of cake we took
when no one was looking
or of our sisters' faces in the moonlight.

A select few of us may be put on display,
skulls cracked open behind thick glass, labelled,
stomachs scraped to determine our diets.

We will be cured of ourselves, finally.
How primitive we will seem to those who look back,
how irrelevant to those who look forward —
if they pattern our lives they'll trace
only how far they've come.

Recipe

On the table there is butter, salt, potato —
no good reason for this to speak of history,

of *oíche mhaith*, of *ocras*, and the rest of that language
living under the stairs of your ancestors' childhoods.

You were given English voices, sounds they feared
roll off your tongue. The old words were schoolwork —

the ache of reciting meaningless prayers, dead
in your throat, you heard only wind and loose change.

In all those classrooms teachers said *arís! arís! arís!*
as if you could hammer a language back into its people.

Now it's evening, slip from under the thumb
of consciousness, imagine a woman who looks like you.

On her table there is butter, salt, potato — steam rising
in the cold air. Though you say potato and she says *fataí*,

though you say thanks and she says *buíochas le Dia*,
your tongues make the same shape as you swallow.

Intrusion

Running early to avoid the heat
I saw a dead snake, body baking
on the pavement, growing darker,
flatter by the hour like some shadow
a child might peel from the grit.

Surprised by its presence, half afraid
the roadside grass might begin to hiss,
or another would appear — fierce, intelligent.
I didn't know the word for snake
or how to say, *Help, I've been bitten.*

I've gone out knowing nothing,
oblivious in strange landscapes,
the trees, the roads, the mountains,
places for me to run through.
All these years, all these passings,
my body deaf to its surroundings,
striding over whole histories.

That I could go out one morning,
expecting to find my way, safely,
and to return as I did, as I do,
to check a word, a phrase, as if
the only question is survival.

Note to Self for When the Crisis Is Over

Do not let me worry the days into blunt ends,
none of it can be corralled into neat lists
or spreadsheets counting targets, budgets, words.

Here are the blank squares of my old plans.
Look, how easily it all fell apart,
leaving only time, only me, only him.

When it all gets busy again
may I give myself time to do the easy things well
like lying quietly in the mornings, listening

to the faint sound of his breathing, in and out,
how lovely it is to close my eyes and touch
his body soft with sleep in our bed.

The Snow Spirit

I've only seen snow like this
in films, falling in sheets
over all the greys, browns,
pavements hidden
beneath its forceful quiet.

A Yorkshire Terrier
turns her face upwards,
her yellow raincoat,
a dash of vibrant colour,
hind legs lost in the drift,
paws in red booties.

Something so irresistible
about those booties,
red dots punctuating
the quiet.

A woman tugs her lead,
maybe work, maybe emails.

But this creature is resolute,
she will have —
snow going kiss, kiss,
wind going wahoosh, wahoosh,
footsteps going munch, munch.

It's delicious.

She eats it up
in big white mouthfuls,
body shivering
as snow melts in her throat,
becoming one
with her tiny dog cells.

Her spirit takes up
the whole street.

Visitor

Let me bring the girl I once was here,
just for a visit. I'll show her the whole place —
cupboards full of blues, greens, a fridge full of food,
brown bear still propped up against the pillows.
She'll curl up in this quiet world, and I'll tell her
how one day she will collapse at your feet, exhausted.
She won't believe me, but I'll tell her anyway,
about the sleet, the concrete, the creaky gate,
how you lift her from the cold, hard ground,
her full-grown body limp in your arms.
She won't like that one bit. I'll say you give her
tea, blankets, and she will make a childish face.
I'll persist. It seems urgent that she should know
there's a language she does not yet speak,
full of gentleness. I'll tell her about the morning,
years from where she stands, when you hold her
for as long as it takes to stop the trembling.

Mirage

Have you ever felt your life
get up and circle the room,
take in each faint detail, then fade.
It's as if you surface in one place
and then must go to a house
on a street with a strange name
where the sea gathers and glistens.

Somewhere inside you is a child
standing where sand meets water,
the edge of your known universe,
dipping in one toe, then the other,
heels barely touching dry land.
Somewhere inside is also a parent,
further up the shore, neck deep
in a hole they've dug for themselves.

It's an old game, a staple
of beaches and bizarre traditions
enacted from memory or movie reels,
only to realize here you are, turning
the hourglass without knowing why.
Who knows what the world wants?
Only that it asks and there are hours
when you try to answer. Maybe
all lives are a series of responses
to impossible questions. The sand
spilling isn't time, but how
you remember: grains, grief.

It's astonishing, really, the distance
between you and your days —
buried or half-buried,
where are you when evening colours
the clouds with its rough hands?

Can you keep in your mind
the parent, the sand? Do you see
the child blurring on the shoreline,
speaking seagull and jellyfish,
begging the day to remain open?

Acknowledgements and Notes

Acknowledgements are due to the editors of the following publications where some of these poems, or versions of them, were published first: *The Antigonish Review, Banshee, Days of Clear Light* (Salmon Poetry), *Dodging the Rain, Flare, I Traveled West: Poets on Place & Belonging* (Contemporary Irish Arts Centre Los Angeles), *Local Wonders* (Dedalus Press), *Poetry Ireland Review* and *Poetry Pause* (The League of Canadian Poets).

I also wish to acknowledge the support of the Irish Poetry Archive's Diaspora Poet Series where several of these poems are archived in video and handwritten format.

I'm deeply thankful to Peter Fallon for the insight, humour and tact with which he edited this manuscript. I'm also grateful to the team at The Gallery Press who helped to make this book possible.

I am grateful to Anne Tannam for her generous support, friendship and thoughtful edits throughout the preparation of this manuscript. She is responsible for some of the best life and writing advice I've received.

Much love and thanks to Fiona Bolger for always showing up for Friday morning workshops across oceans; she kept me sane through years of homesickness. I'm also grateful for her generosity and thoughts on the manuscript.

Thanks to Alicia Byrne Keane, K Srilata, Özgecan Kesici, Lynn Harding, Mahsa Ebadpour, Lucy Carragher and Lea Chambers for their thoughtful notes over the years on various poems and versions of the manuscript.

Thank you also to the Monday night writers at the Writers Collective of Canada. They heard some of this work in its roughest and earliest form.

For keeping in touch despite so much distance I'm grateful for the friendship and support of Emmylou Arnaud, Gemma Creagh, Lotte Krause, Casey Armstrong, Rosamund Taylor, Bernadette Gallagher, Thekiso B Thekiso, Ola Kubiak, Rachel O'Connor and Phil Lynch.

My most heartfelt thanks to Stephen Murphy for always being there for me. I wish to thank him not only for our life together and the support he gives me but also for his keen eye for a half-truth.

Sincere thanks to The Arts Council of Ireland for a Bursary in Literature (2022).

page 17   *Peadar Pluaise* is an Irish school reader published by Folens that included a reference to nettle soup.

page 18   My mother often took us across fields to look at ruins and deserted houses in improbable places. Though they may not have been famine houses there were often suggestions that they could be.

page 19   Boreen is Hiberno-English for *bóithrín*, a diminutive of *bóthar*, the Irish for road whose etymology is *bó* and *thar* meaning cow and over, across or abreast. It refers to a lane or little road where there is only room for one car to pass.

page 25   Based on an old fairytale which has taken many forms across many countries. Perhaps the most definitive version is *The Wild Swans* by Hans Christian Andersen.

page 26   *Mallacht* is Irish for curse.

page 29   *Aimsir* is Irish for weather.

page 32   The title is Hiberno-English for the Irish *murúch*, a mermaid or merman. The Silvermines is a hilly area near Nenagh, Co Tipperary.

page 38   The hunt was when people on horses with hounds went out to kill foxes in the fields.

page 45   Each Irish word is accompanied by its translation. Though I've always been called Alvy my name is Ailbhe on my birth certificate. I first heard Ailbhe when I started school.

page 48   My local church was in Gortanumera, Co Galway. In the 1990s it was still divided by gender.

page 55   This refers to a note I found in an old edition of *Heart Songs* (*The Intimate Diaries of Young Girls*) edited by Laurel Holliday. I found the book and its unlikely bookmark in a local secondhand bookshop when I was living in Vancouver, Canada.

page 57   This poem refers to Karpathos Island, Greece.

page 62   My grandmother was Nancy Carragher (*née* O'Toole), originally from Inishturk, Co Mayo. She spent her final years in Corrandulla, Co Galway, and was buried in Aughavale Cemetery in Westport, Co Mayo.

page 75 *Oíche mhaith* is Irish for good night, *ocras* for hunger, *arís* for again, *fataí* for potatoes (in Connemara) and *buíochas le Dia* for thanks be to God.

page 76 This poem is set in Goheung, South Korea, where I taught English in 2017-2018.

page 78 This poem refers to the first big snow I witnessed while living in Toronto, Canada.